Table of Contents

Introduction

- Why Leadership Skills are Crucial

- Differences Between Leading and Managing

Chapter 1: The Role of a Leader

- Responsibilities of a Leader

- Qualities of an Effective Leader

Chapter 2: Communication and Empathy

- The Art of Listening

- Empathy as the Key to Employee Motivation

Chapter 3: Employee Development and Promotion

- Recognizing and Utilizing Individual Strengths

- Mentoring and Coaching: Advancing Your Employees

Chapter 4: Conflict Management and Problem Solving

- Dealing with Team Conflicts
- Creative Approaches to Problem Solving

Chapter 5: Motivation and Teamwork

- Intrinsic vs. Extrinsic Motivation
- Team-building Strategies That Work

Chapter 6: Time Management and Efficiency

- Setting Priorities and Using Time Wisely
- Delegation: Effectively Distributing Tasks

Chapter 7: Change Management and Innovation

- Handling Changes in the Organization
- Fostering Innovation and Creativity Within the Team

Chapter 8: Leadership in Practice

- Case Studies of Successful Leaders

- Tips for Continuous Development as a Leader

Conclusion

- The Significance of Value-based Leadership

- Challenges and Opportunities for Future Leaders

Introduction

Why Leadership Competence is Crucial

Leadership competence stands as one of the central pillars for the success of a company or an organization. It not only influences the performance of employees but also shapes the organizational culture and long-term success. In this section, we will illuminate the reasons why leadership competence is so crucial and how it impacts various aspects of a company.

1. Employee Motivation and Engagement

One of the key functions of a leader is to motivate employees and foster their commitment to the organization. Leadership competence enables understanding and addressing the needs and expectations of employees, creating a positive work environment where employees feel valued and engaged.

Motivated employees are more productive, work efficiently, and significantly contribute to the company's success. They are also more likely to stay with the company for longer, reducing turnover and ensuring continuity in teams.

2. Achieving Organizational Goals

Leaders play a vital role in aligning employees with organizational goals. They establish clear objectives and priorities, communicate them effectively, and ensure the entire team works towards them. Competent leaders understand how to optimize resources and remove obstacles to ensure goal attainment.

3. Employee Development

Leadership competence is also demonstrated in the ability to develop and nurture employees. Through regular feedback, coaching, and mentoring, leaders support the professional growth of their team members. This not only leads to higher employee satisfaction but also ensures that the company possesses the necessary skills and talents for the future.

4. Conflict Resolution and Team Dynamics

Conflicts are inevitable in any work environment. However, a competent leader knows how to identify and constructively resolve conflicts in a timely manner. This promotes positive team dynamics and prevents conflicts from becoming prolonged issues that strain the work atmosphere.

5. Fostering Innovation

Leaders are also responsible for promoting a culture of innovation and creativity. They encourage employees to contribute new ideas and take risks. This is crucial for a company's adaptability to changing market conditions and long-term success.

6. Shaping Organizational Culture

The leaders of an organization significantly contribute to shaping and influencing the organizational culture. Their values, behaviors, and decisions serve as examples for employees. A competent leader advocates for a corporate culture based on trust, openness, integrity, and respect.

7. Customer Orientation

The way leaders guide their employees directly impacts customer satisfaction. Satisfied and engaged employees are better equipped to provide excellent customer service, fostering customer loyalty and enhancing the company's reputation.

8. Crisis Management

In turbulent times or amid crises, leadership competence is particularly important. Leaders must be able to act calmly and effectively to guide the company through difficult phases. They need to make clear decisions and maintain the trust of employees and stakeholders.

Leadership competence is undeniably crucial for the success of a company. It not only influences the performance and motivation of employees but also the organizational culture, innovation capability, and ability to adapt to changing market conditions. Companies that invest in the development of their leaders are better positioned to achieve long-term success and thrive in a competitive environment. Therefore, the development of leadership competence should be a priority for every company.

The Differences Between Leading and Managing

In the world of business management, the terms "leading" and "managing" are often intertwined or even used synonymously. However, in reality, leading and managing are two distinct concepts, each with its own tasks and requirements. To be an effective leader, it is crucial to understand these differences and recognize when to lead and when to manage.

1. Leading is Visionary, Managing is Organizing

The central difference between leading and managing lies in the orientation of tasks. Leading is visionary. A leader has a clear vision of the future and works towards guiding the team or organization in that direction. The focus of leading is on long-term goals, strategic alignment, and inspiring employees.

A manager, on the other hand, is an organizer. They concentrate on daily operations and processes to ensure that work is done efficiently. The manager ensures that resources are allocated correctly, tasks are completed, and goals are achieved within the framework of pre-established plans.

2. Leading Inspires, Managing Controls

Another significant difference lies in the way of interacting with employees. A leader inspires their employees to give their best. They create a vision that excites employees and motivates them to achieve this vision together. Leaders who lead are often communicative, empathetic, and inspirational.

A manager, however, focuses more on controlling workflows. They monitor performance, ensure that policies are followed, and take action when things do not go as planned. Managers are typically precise, structured, and place great emphasis on compliance.

3. Leading Thinks Long-Term, Managing Thinks Short-Term

Leadership and management also differ in their time horizon. A leader thinks long-term. They plan for the future and invest in employee development to achieve long-term goals. Leaders often have a long-term strategy in mind and are willing to make short-term sacrifices for long-term success.

A manager, on the other hand, is often oriented towards short-term results. They work on completing current tasks and ensuring that daily operations run smoothly. Managers have less time and space for long-term planning and must focus on addressing current challenges.

4. Leading Delegates, Managing Controls

Differences also arise in task distribution. A leader is willing to delegate responsibility and trust their employees. They encourage employees to act independently and find solutions. Leaders understand that they cannot do everything themselves and that developing employees is crucial to success.

A manager, on the other hand, often retains control over many tasks. They tend to oversee every decision and ensure that things follow their plan. This can lead to employees feeling less autonomous and having less room for creativity.

Chapter 1

The Role of a Leader

The Responsibilities of a Leader

The role of a leader in an organization or a company is crucial for the success and efficiency of the team or department. But what exactly are the responsibilities of a leader? In this section, we will provide a deep insight into the tasks and responsibilities of a leader and highlight how to lead people, not just manage them.

Vision and Strategic Alignment

One of the most important responsibilities of a leader is to create a clear vision and strategic alignment for the team or organization. This involves defining long-term goals and ensuring that all team members understand where the journey is headed. The vision should be inspiring and motivate employees to commit to common goals.

Leaders must also ensure that the strategy to implement the vision is developed and communicated. This includes setting priorities, allocating resources, and creating a clear action plan.

Employee Leadership and Development

One of the fundamental responsibilities of a leader is to lead the employees. This includes selecting, hiring, and onboarding new team members, setting clear expectations and goals, and supporting professional development.

Leaders should be able to recognize the strengths and weaknesses of their employees and provide them with the opportunity to develop their skills. This can be achieved through regular feedback, coaching, and mentoring.

Communication and Teamwork

Effective communication is central to the success of a team or organization. Leaders must be able to communicate clearly and transparently to ensure that all employees have the same information and are working in the same direction.

Promoting teamwork is also a crucial responsibility of a leader. This means creating an environment where employees collaborate, exchange ideas, and learn from each other. A team that works well together is generally more productive and creative.

Conflict Resolution and Problem Solving

Conflicts and issues are inevitable in any organization. A leader must be able to recognize and constructively resolve conflicts. This requires empathy, good communication skills, and the ability to act fairly and justly.

Problems should not be avoided but actively addressed. Leaders are often responsible for removing obstacles, providing resources, and finding solutions to ensure that work runs smoothly.

Motivation and Employee Engagement

Employee motivation is a key aspect of a team's success. Leaders should be able to motivate and inspire their employees. This can be achieved through recognition, reward systems, clear goal setting, and creating a positive work environment.

Employee engagement means that employees identify with their job and the company and are willing to put in extra effort to contribute to success. Leaders have the responsibility to create an environment where employees enjoy working and give their best.

Time Management and Efficiency

A leader must be able to manage their time efficiently and set priorities. This means distinguishing important tasks from less important ones and ensuring that resources are utilized optimally.

Delegation is another important skill in time management. Leaders should be able to delegate tasks to the right people in the team to distribute the workload and ensure that all tasks are completed on time.

Change Management and Innovation

In a constantly changing business world, change management is crucial. Leaders must be able to recognize, plan, and implement changes. This requires the ability to guide employees through changes and ensure that they can adapt to new circumstances.

Promoting innovation and creativity is also a vital responsibility. Leaders should create an environment where new ideas are welcome and employees are encouraged to develop innovative solutions.

Ethics and Integrity

A leader must have high ethical integrity and serve as a role model for their employees. This means acting honestly and transparently, building trust, and living the company's values.

Ethics and integrity are crucial to gaining the trust of employees and stakeholders and protecting the company's reputation.

The responsibilities of a leader are diverse and demanding. An effective leader must be able to create a vision, lead and develop employees, communicate effectively, resolve conflicts, motivate employees, manage time efficiently, manage change, promote innovation, and maintain ethical standards. These responsibilities are crucial for the success of a team or organization and require a high level of leadership competence and commitment. In the following chapters, we will delve deeper into these topics and explore how to lead people, not just manage them.

Leading is Coaching, Managing is Supervising

Another significant difference concerns the role in employee development. A leader often acts as a coach. They support the individual development of their employees, recognize their strengths and weaknesses, and help them reach their full potential. Leaders are usually interested in promoting and inspiring their employees.

A manager, however, is more of a supervisor. They evaluate performance, set expectations, and monitor compliance with rules and regulations. Managers can focus more on maintaining the status quo and fulfilling duties.

The differences between leading and managing are subtle but crucial for the success of a leader. An effective leader must be able to switch between these roles depending on the situation. In many cases, a combination of leadership and management is required to meet the diverse demands in the work environment. The art lies in finding the right balance between these approaches and using them at the right time. A deeper understanding of these differences enables leaders to lead more effectively and guide their teams to success, rather than just managing them.

The Characteristics of an Effective Leader

Being an effective leader is much more than just a title or a position. It requires specific traits and qualities that go beyond mere task and employee management. In this chapter, we will examine the essential characteristics of an effective leader and highlight how to lead people, not just manage them.

Vision and Goal Orientation

One of the most important traits of an effective leader is the ability to have a clear vision and define the goals of the team or organization. This vision serves as a guiding star and inspires employees to commit to common objectives. An effective leader knows where they want to lead the team and sets clear goals and priorities to achieve this vision.

Communication Skills

Good communication is crucial for successful leadership. A leader can not only communicate clearly and understandably but also listen and take employees' needs and concerns seriously. Open and honest communication builds trust and fosters a positive work atmosphere.

Empathy and Social Intelligence

Empathy, the ability to understand the thoughts and feelings of others, is an important trait of a leader. It allows understanding the needs and expectations of employees better and responding appropriately. Social intelligence, the ability to shape and maintain interpersonal relationships, is also crucial to creating a harmonious and productive team environment.

Decision-Making and Problem-Solving Skills

Leaders often need to make quick and wise decisions. An effective leader has the ability to gather information, weigh it carefully, and make bold decisions when necessary. They are also capable of recognizing problems and finding creative solutions to overcome obstacles.

Responsibility and Integrity

Responsibility and integrity are fundamental traits of a leader. They act according to ethical principles, are reliable, and keep promises. A leader takes responsibility for their actions and the results of their team.

Motivation and Inspiration

A leader is a motivator and inspirer. They encourage employees to give their best and create an environment where engagement and passion are fostered. An inspiring leader can motivate employees to go above and beyond and achieve great things together.

Teamwork and Collaboration

A leader values teamwork and collaboration. They promote a culture where team members collaborate, exchange ideas, and learn from one another. They recognize the strengths and weaknesses of each team member and ensure that skills are utilized optimally.

Adaptability and Resilience

In a constantly changing business world, adaptability is of great importance. An effective leader is flexible and willing to adapt to new challenges and changes. They also show resilience by standing firm in difficult times and supporting their employees.

Delegation Skills

Delegation is an important trait of a leader. They recognize that they cannot do everything themselves and are willing to delegate responsibility to qualified employees. This allows distributing the workload and promoting employees.

Willingness to Learn and Continuous Improvement

An effective leader never stops learning. They are willing to acquire new skills and knowledge and continuously develop themselves. They follow trends and developments in their field and adjust their leadership strategies accordingly.

Self-Reflection and Self-Awareness

Self-reflection is an important trait that allows a leader to critically question and improve their own behavior and decisions. Self-awareness helps recognize one's strengths and weaknesses and stay true to oneself.

Patience and Perseverance

The path to success is often filled with challenges and setbacks. A leader shows patience and perseverance to hold onto their goals despite difficulties and encourages their employees to do the same.

The traits of a leader are diverse and demanding. A successful leader combines a clear vision, excellent communication skills, empathy, decision-making ability, responsibility, motivation, teamwork, adaptability, delegation skills, willingness to learn, self-reflection, self-awareness, patience, and perseverance. These traits form the foundation for strong and inspiring leadership.

It is important to note that nobody is a perfect leader by nature, and the development of these traits is a continuous journey. By consciously focusing on developing these traits and working on your own leadership skills, you can learn and successfully implement the art of leadership. In the following chapters, we will explore specific strategies and techniques for developing these traits and help you become an effective leader who leads people, not just manages them.

Chapter 2

Communication and Empathy

The Art of Listening – Key Skill of a Successful Leader

A leader is one of the central figures in any company or organization. Their influence extends not only to the business processes but also to the employees. But how can one become a successful leader who not only manages but truly leads people? One of the crucial elements is the art of listening.

In this chapter, we will delve into the significance of listening in leadership. We will illuminate why listening is a key skill for successful leaders, how it strengthens interpersonal relationships, and how you can master the art of listening to enhance your leadership qualities.

Why Is Listening So Important for Leaders?

Listening might appear as a self-evident skill at first glance, but in the realm of leadership, it is one of the most underestimated yet crucial qualities. Here are some reasons why listening is of great importance for leaders:

Building Trust and Respect

By actively listening to your employees, you show them that you respect them and value their opinions and concerns. This fosters trust and respect, two key components of successful leadership.

Clear Communication

Good listening allows you to precisely understand your employees' messages. You can avoid misunderstandings and ensure that information is conveyed clearly and accurately.

Problem Solving

Employees often contribute valuable knowledge and ideas to problem-solving. By listening to them, you can benefit from their experiences and insights, finding better solutions together.

Employee Engagement and Motivation

Feeling heard and understood is a powerful motivator. Employees who feel heard are often more engaged and motivated to contribute to the company's goals.

Conflict Resolution

Conflicts are inevitable in any organization. Good listening enables leaders to identify and constructively resolve conflicts before they escalate.

Promoting Innovation

By listening to your employees and encouraging their ideas, you contribute to the culture of innovation in your company. Creative ideas often arise from open dialogue and an environment where employees feel heard.

Improving Workplace Relationships

Good listening strengthens interpersonal relationships in the workplace. Employees who know their leader is listening to them are more willing to communicate openly and constructively.

The Art of Active Listening

Now that we understand the importance of listening for leaders, let's delve into the art of active listening. Active listening is more than just passively hearing words; it is a conscious and engaged form of listening aimed at fully understanding the speaker's thoughts, feelings, and needs. Here are some key aspects of the art of active listening:

Attention and Focus

To actively listen, you must direct your full attention to the speaker. Eliminate distractions and ensure you maintain eye contact. Focus on what the speaker is saying rather than thinking about what you will say next.

Empathy

Empathy is a central component of active listening. Put yourself in the speaker's shoes and try to see the world from their perspective. This means not only hearing the words but also recognizing the emotions and motivations behind them.

Avoiding Judgement

Active listening requires setting aside your own biases and judgments. Avoid making premature judgments or interrupting the speaker to express your own opinions. Instead, patiently listen until the speaker has fully expressed their thoughts.

Providing Feedback

To ensure you have understood the speaker correctly, it is helpful to provide regular feedback. This can be in the form of summaries or follow-up questions. For example, you could say, "Let me make sure I understand. You mean that..."

Asking Open-Ended Questions

Open-ended questions encourage the speaker to provide more detailed answers and allow you to learn more about their thoughts and feelings. Ask questions like "Could you tell me more about that?" or "How do you feel about it?"

Body Language

Your body language plays a crucial role in active listening. Show the speaker that you are attentive and interested through nods, eye contact, and an open posture. This encourages the speaker to open up and feel heard.

Patience

Active listening requires patience. It may take some time for the speaker to fully express their thoughts. Avoid jumping to hasty conclusions or rushing to conclude the conversation. Patient listening helps establish a deeper connection.

Respect and Acknowledgment

Show respect and acknowledgment for the speaker and their opinions. Even if you disagree, it is essential to respect others' viewpoints and make them feel valued.

Benefits of Active Listening for Leaders

Applying the art of active listening offers numerous benefits for leaders:

Improved Relationships

Active listening enhances interpersonal relationships by promoting trust and connection. It also helps avoid or resolve conflicts.

More Effective Communication

Active listening leads to clearer and more effective communication. Misunderstandings and miscommunication are reduced as the speaker feels better understood.

Better Problem-Solving

Through active listening, problems and challenges can be addressed more effectively. By understanding others' perspectives, better solutions can be found collaboratively.

Expanded Knowledge

Active listening allows you to learn from others' experiences and knowledge. By absorbing others' thoughts and ideas, you expand your knowledge and perspective.

Professional Success

In a professional context, active listening is a key skill for success. It helps understand customers, colleagues, and superiors better, leading to better decision-making.

Conflict Resolution

Active listening is a valuable tool for conflict resolution. It enables identifying the root causes of conflicts and finding solutions together.

Empathy and Compassion

Active listening fosters empathy and compassion. By empathizing with others' thoughts and feelings, you develop a deeper understanding and appreciation for their perspective.

The art of listening is an invaluable skill for leaders. It enables building better relationships, communicating more effectively, personal growth, and professional success. Active listening requires attention, empathy, and commitment, but the rewards are manifold. By consciously focusing on developing this skill and working on your listening competence, you can master the art of listening and become a more effective and empathetic leader. In the following chapters, we will discuss specific strategies and techniques to enhance your listening skills and help you implement this key competency in your leadership practice.

Empathy as the Key to Employee Motivation

The Art of Leading People, Not Managing Them

Modern leadership has undergone significant changes over the past few decades, shifting away from authoritarian top-down management towards a more cooperative and employee-centered approach. In this section, we will delve deeply into one of the key aspects of this transformation: empathy as the key to employee motivation.

The ability to show empathy is not just a desirable trait for leaders; it is increasingly becoming a prerequisite for successful management. In this chapter, we will illuminate how empathy can be applied in leadership to motivate employees, foster engagement, and positively influence the work environment.

What is Empathy?

Before we explore empathy in leadership in depth, let's first understand what empathy truly means. Empathy is the ability to put oneself in the feelings, thoughts, and perspectives of other people. It goes beyond mere understanding; it means genuinely stepping into the other person's shoes and sensing their emotions and needs.

Empathy is a multidimensional concept encompassing various aspects:

Emotional Empathy

This refers to the ability to feel and resonate with another person's emotions. For instance, if an employee is frustrated or excited, as an empathetic leader, you can empathize with these emotions.

Cognitive Empathy

This involves understanding another person's perspective and thoughts intellectually. You strive to see the world from their viewpoint, comprehending their motivations and considerations better.

Empathetic Action

This is the implementation of empathy into concrete actions. It means taking appropriate actions based on your empathetic insights to acknowledge and respond to your employees' needs and emotions.

Empathy is not just an innate ability; it can be developed and improved. Cultivating empathy in leadership requires attention, mindfulness, and practice.

Why is Empathy Important in Leadership?

Empathy in leadership has profound effects on employee motivation and well-being as well as the company's success. Here are some reasons why empathy is crucial in leadership:

Building Trust

Empathetic leaders build trust with their employees. When employees feel that their leader understands and respects their needs and feelings, they are more willing to trust.

Employee Retention

Empathetic leaders often experience higher employee retention rates. When employees feel heard and understood, they are less likely to leave the company.

Boosting Engagement

Empathy enhances employee engagement. When they feel that their leader takes their concerns seriously and addresses their needs, they are more motivated and engaged in their work.

Conflict Resolution

Empathetic leaders are better equipped to resolve conflicts. They can understand the perspectives of conflicting parties and address conflicts in a way that is acceptable to all involved.

Promoting Innovation

Empathetic leadership fosters openness to new ideas and innovations. Employees are more willing to suggest creative solutions when they feel supported by their leader.

Positive Work Atmosphere

Empathy contributes to a positive work atmosphere. Employees feel more comfortable and motivated in an environment where empathy is present.

Customer Satisfaction

Empathetic leadership also impacts customer satisfaction. Employees who feel valued are more likely to recognize and cater to customer needs effectively.

How Can Empathy be Applied in Leadership?

Applying empathy in leadership requires conscious effort and a systematic approach. Here are some steps to implement empathy in your leadership practice:

Active Listening

Begin by actively listening when your employees speak. Focus entirely on the speaker, avoid distractions, and do not interrupt. Provide feedback to ensure you have understood correctly.

Perspective-Taking

Try to see things from your employees' perspective. Consider how they might feel in a given situation and take their viewpoint into account when making decisions and taking actions.

Empathetic Questioning

Ask open-ended questions to learn more about your employees' thoughts and feelings. Inquire about their opinions, concerns, and suggestions. Show genuine interest in their responses.

Time and Attention

Take time for personal conversations with your employees. Listen to their stories and demonstrate your concern for their well-being. This can involve both professional and personal matters.

Empathetic Communication

Express empathy in your communication. Use phrases like "I understand this is a challenge for you" or "I'm sorry you're feeling this way." Show compassion and understanding.

Feedback and Recognition

Acknowledge and appreciate your employees' achievements and efforts. Provide constructive feedback and show appreciation for their work.

Offering Support

Offer assistance and support when employees are in difficult situations. Show that you are there for them and willing to provide help.

Authenticity

Empathy must be authentic. Pretending to be empathetic is of little use. It is important to show genuine interest and true compassion.

Challenges of Empathy in Leadership

While empathy in leadership offers many benefits, it can also pose challenges. Some leaders might hesitate to show empathy, fearing they will be perceived as too lenient or uncertain. However, it is crucial to understand that empathy does not signify weakness; it is a strength.

Another challenge is finding the right balance between empathy and objectivity. Leaders still need to make objective decisions and pursue the company's goals while being empathetic. This requires finesse and judgment.

Lastly, empathy in leadership can also be emotionally taxing. Leaders who strongly empathize with their employees' feelings can become emotionally exhausted themselves. It is important to practice self-care and seek support when needed.

Empathy is a critical key to employee motivation and successful leadership. It builds trust, promotes engagement, and enhances the work atmosphere. Empathetic leaders are better able to resolve conflicts, foster innovation, and increase the satisfaction of both employees and customers.

However, empathy is not a superficial gesture; it requires genuine interest and commitment. It can be learned and developed, and it is a quality that is increasingly gaining importance in modern leadership.

Chapter 3

Employee Development and Promotion

Recognizing and Utilizing Individual Strengths – The Art of Personalized Leadership

In today's business world, characterized by diversity and dynamism, it is crucial for leaders to recognize and harness the individual strengths of their employees. This section focuses on the topic of "Recognizing and Utilizing Employees' Individual Strengths" and demonstrates how, as a leader, you can fully leverage the potential of your team members to achieve success together.

Why are Individual Strengths Important?

Recognizing and utilizing the individual strengths of each employee offers numerous advantages that impact the entire team and organization. Here are some reasons why this is crucial:

Increased Productivity

Employees who can apply their strengths at work are generally more productive. They complete tasks more efficiently and effectively, leading to better outcomes.

Motivation and Engagement

When employees feel that their skills and strengths are valued, they are more motivated and engaged. They feel appreciated and are willing to contribute more to common goals.

Improved Job Satisfaction

Employees who can use their strengths typically experience higher job satisfaction. They feel more comfortable in their roles and are less frustrated.

Expertise Development

Individual strengths can lead to expertise and knowledge in specific areas. When employees have the opportunity to develop their strengths, they can become valuable resources for the company.

Enhanced Teamwork

In a team where individual strengths are recognized and utilized, members often complement each other better. This leads to more effective collaboration and a harmonious work environment.

Promotion of Innovation

Employees with diverse strengths can develop innovative solutions to complex problems. The combination of different strengths can lead to creative ideas.

Employee Retention

Companies that foster the individual strengths of their employees often have higher employee retention rates. Employees are less likely to leave the company when they can tap into their potential.

The Role of the Leader in Identifying and Utilizing Individual Strengths

Identifying and utilizing individual strengths starts with the leader. As a leader, you play a central role in creating an environment where your employees can discover, develop, and apply their strengths. Here are some ways in which you can achieve this:

Identifying Individual Strengths

Begin by identifying the strengths of each employee in your team. This can be done through discussions, observation, and targeted questioning. Ask your employees in which areas they feel particularly strong and where they have achieved their greatest successes.

Promoting Strengths

After identifying your employees' strengths, actively promote them. Provide opportunities for them to take on projects or tasks that align with their strengths. Encourage them to further develop in these areas.

Assigning Tasks

Tailor the tasks and responsibilities in your team to the individual strengths of your employees. Distribute the work in a way that allows each person to excel in their respective areas.

Training and Development

Offer training and development opportunities tailored to your employees' strengths. This can include both formal training and informal learning.

Feedback and Recognition

Provide regular feedback and recognition for your employees' achievements in their areas of strength. Show that you appreciate their efforts and acknowledge their successes.

Mentoring and Coaching

Encourage experienced employees to mentor and coach younger colleagues. This allows experienced employees to pass on their knowledge and strengths while promoting the development of younger employees.

Appreciating Diversity

Recognize that diversity in your employees' strengths and skills is a valuable asset. Appreciate the differences and foster a culture that respects and supports each employee's individual strengths.

Case Study: The Power of Individual Strengths in Practice

To illustrate the importance of individual strengths in leadership, let's look at a case study:

Company X

Company X is a mid-sized technology company specializing in software solutions. The CEO, Thomas, recognized the need to better leverage his employees' individual strengths to enhance the company's innovation capabilities.

Step 1: Strengths Identification

Thomas started by having conversations with his employees to identify their strengths and interests. He realized that some employees had a strong talent for creative solutions, while others were particularly analytical and structured.

Step 2: Strengths Promotion

Based on the identified strengths, Thomas adjusted the project teams. Creative employees were assigned to innovation projects, while analytical employees worked on process optimization and quality assurance.

Step 3: Training and Development

Thomas invested in training programs tailored to individual strengths. Creative employees attended design thinking workshops, while analytical employees received training in data analysis.

Step 4: Feedback and Recognition

Thomas provided regular feedback and recognition for his employees' progress and achievements. He emphasized the importance of their strengths to the company's success.

Outcome

By harnessing his employees' individual strengths, Company X was able to develop innovative solutions that gained recognition in the industry. Employees were motivated and engaged because they could apply their strengths in their work.

Challenges in Utilizing Individual Strengths

While leveraging individual strengths offers many benefits, there are also challenges to overcome. Here are some of the most common challenges:

Identification

Accurately identifying each employee's individual strengths can be a challenge. It requires time and attention to understand each person's strengths.

Resources

Tailoring tasks and training initiatives to individual strengths requires additional resources and planning.

Balance

It is essential to strike a balance between utilizing individual strengths and organizational goals. Sometimes compromises need to be made.

Communication

Clear communication is crucial to ensure that all employees understand why specific decisions are made and how their strengths fit into the overall strategy of the company.

Utilizing employees' individual strengths is a crucial factor in a company's success. Leaders play a central role in identifying and promoting these strengths. By recognizing and utilizing your employees' individual strengths, you can not only enhance performance and productivity but also improve your employees' motivation and satisfaction.

It takes time, attention, and planning to make individual strengths a focal point of your leadership, but the results are worth it. Individual strengths are the building blocks for innovation, engagement, and long-term success in the modern business world.

Mentoring and Coaching: How to Advance Your Employees

In today's business world, characterized by constant change and rising demands, the role of a leader is much more than just managing tasks and processes. Successful leaders understand that developing their employees is crucial to ensuring long-term success. In this section, we will delve into the topics of mentoring and coaching and show you how to utilize these powerful tools to support and promote your employees on their professional journey.

The Significance of Mentoring and Coaching in Modern Leadership

The business world has undergone significant changes in recent years. With the increasing complexity of the work environment and the constant evolution of technology and processes, leaders face new challenges. One of the key aspects of successful leadership in today's time is the development and promotion of employees.

Mentoring and coaching are two key approaches that leaders can use to drive this development. They provide opportunities for individual support and guidance to optimize employees' skills and potential.

The Basics of Mentoring and Coaching

Before delving deeper into mentoring and coaching, it is important to understand the basics:

What is Mentoring?

Mentoring is a long-term process where an experienced employee (the mentor) guides and supports a less experienced employee (the mentee). The mentor shares their knowledge, experience, and insights and provides support for professional development. The primary goal of mentoring is the personal and professional growth of the mentee.

What is Coaching?

Coaching, on the other hand, is a short- to medium-term process where a coach assists a coachee in developing specific skills or achieving certain goals. Coaching is often focused on specific challenges or developmental needs and can occur in various areas such as communication, leadership, or conflict resolution.

Both approaches have their place in leadership, and the choice between mentoring and coaching depends on the individual needs of your employees and the goals of your organization.

The Benefits of Mentoring and Coaching in Leadership

Integrating mentoring and coaching into your leadership practices offers numerous advantages:

Leadership Development

Mentoring and coaching enable you to identify and nurture emerging leaders. They allow you to build a pipeline of talented leaders ready to move into higher positions.

Knowledge Transfer

Experienced employees can pass down their knowledge and experience to younger generations. This helps preserve valuable company knowledge and ensures it is not lost.

Employee Development

Mentoring and coaching contribute to the continuous development of your employees. They allow employees to learn new skills, deepen existing ones, and advance their careers.

Motivation and Retention

Employees who feel supported and promoted by their supervisors are often more motivated and more strongly attached to the company. They are willing to contribute to the company's success.

Conflict Resolution

Coaching can also be used to resolve conflicts and improve interpersonal relationships in the workplace. A coach can help identify conflicts and suggest ways to resolve them.

Enhanced Self-reflection

Through coaching, employees can improve their self-reflection and gain a better understanding of their strengths, weaknesses, and areas for development.

Implementing Mentoring and Coaching in Leadership

Integrating mentoring and coaching into your leadership practices requires a targeted approach. Here are some steps you can follow:

Needs Analysis

Identify the needs of your employees and your organization. Where is mentoring and coaching most urgently required? What developmental goals do you want to achieve?

Selection of Mentors and Coaches

Choose experienced and competent mentors and coaches who meet the needs of your employees. These can be experienced leaders, internal experts, or external consultants.

Assignment of Mentors and Coaches

Assign mentors and coaches to the appropriate employees based on their needs and goals. Ensure that there is good chemistry between the mentor/coach and the mentee/coachee.

Setting Goals

Define clear goals and expectations for the mentoring and coaching program. What do you want participants to achieve in the end? How will success be measured?

Training and Support

Provide training and resources to mentors and coaches to enable them to fulfill their roles effectively. Ensure they have the necessary skills and tools to succeed.

Monitoring and Feedback

Track the progress of the mentoring and coaching program and continuously gather feedback from participants. Adjust the program as needed.

Evaluation and Adaptation

After the program is completed, assess the results and benefits of mentoring and coaching. Based on the insights, make adjustments and further develop the program.

Challenges of Mentoring and Coaching

While mentoring and coaching offer many benefits, there are challenges that need to be overcome:

Time Commitment

Mentoring and coaching require time from both the mentor/coach and the mentee/coachee. This can be a challenge in a busy work environment.

Selecting the Right People

Choosing the right mentors and coaches is crucial. Not every experienced employee automatically makes a good mentor or coach.

Individualization

Each employee has different developmental needs. It requires a personalized approach to ensure that mentoring and coaching are effective.

Resistance to Change

Some employees might resist mentoring and coaching, especially if they feel challenged by their weaknesses or areas for development.

Case Studies and Success Stories

In this chapter, we will explore some case studies and success stories to see how companies have successfully implemented mentoring and coaching to promote employee development and enhance organizational success.

Tips for Successful Implementation

Finally, we will provide practical tips and recommendations for successful implementation of mentoring and coaching in your leadership practices. We will discuss proven strategies on how to use these powerful tools to advance your employees and keep your team on the path to success.

The Power of Mentoring and Coaching in Leadership

Mentoring and coaching are indispensable tools for modern leaders who want to develop and promote their employees. They allow for talent recognition, knowledge transfer, employee development, and strengthen your employees' attachment to the company. With a targeted approach and a clear vision, you can harness the power of mentoring and coaching to make both your employees and your company successful.

Chapter 4

Conflict Management and Problem Solving

Dealing with Team Conflicts: The Art of Conflict Resolution for Leaders

Conflicts are inevitable in any work environment. As a leader, it is your responsibility not only to manage conflicts but also to use them as opportunities for improvement. In this section, we will thoroughly explore the topic of "Dealing with Team Conflicts" and show you how as a leader, you can effectively resolve conflicts to create a harmonious and productive work environment.

The Nature of Team Conflicts

Before addressing conflict resolution, it is important to understand what triggers conflicts within a team and the types of conflicts that can occur:

Causes of Conflicts

Conflicts can arise for various reasons, including differing opinions, interests, values, personalities, and communication issues.

Types of Conflicts

Conflicts can occur at different levels, such as between employees, within teams, or between teams. They can be related to tasks, relationships, or processes.

The Role of the Leader in Conflict Management

Leaders play a central role in handling team conflicts. Here are some key aspects of how you, as a leader, can approach conflicts:

Early Recognition of Conflicts

Be attentive to signs of conflicts, such as team tensions, poor communication, or disrupted work relationships. The earlier you recognize conflicts, the easier they can be resolved.

Promoting Open Communication

Foster an open and trustful communication culture where employees feel safe to express their concerns and opinions. This enables addressing conflicts early on.

Maintaining Neutrality

As a leader, remain neutral and do not take sides. Your role is to act as a mediator and arbitrator.

Mastering Conflict Resolution Techniques

Learn various conflict resolution techniques, such as active listening, mediation, and compromise. These tools can assist you in successfully managing conflicts.

Providing Constructive Feedback

Provide involved employees with constructive feedback to help them reflect on and improve their perspectives and behaviors.

Conflict Resolution Techniques for Leaders

Leaders have various techniques at their disposal for handling conflicts. Here are some proven approaches:

Active Listening

Listen attentively when conflicting parties present their viewpoints. Repeat what you have heard to ensure accurate understanding. This demonstrates respect for their opinions.

Mediation

In some cases, it might be beneficial to involve a neutral third party as a mediator to resolve the conflict. The mediator assists the parties in clarifying their differences and finding mutual solutions.

Compromise

Encourage conflicting parties to collaboratively seek compromises where both sides make concessions. This can help ensure that all parties are satisfied with the resolution.

Conflict Analysis

Examine the roots of the conflict to identify underlying issues. Sometimes, conflicts are merely symptoms of deeper problems.

Conflict Prevention

Ensure clear communication, task distribution, and expectations are established to prevent conflicts from arising in the first place.

Case Studies: Successful Conflict Resolution in Practice

To better understand the concepts of conflict resolution in leadership, let's examine some case studies of successful conflict resolutions in different companies. These examples illustrate how leaders identified and resolved conflicts to improve teamwork and promote business success.

Case Study 1: Conflict Resolution Training

A team leader in a technology company noticed conflicts between two team members, Sarah and John, hindering teamwork. Tensions arose from differing work styles and communication issues. The team leader decided to offer conflict resolution training for the entire team. The training included conflict prevention techniques, active listening, and conflict resolution strategies.

Through the training, Sarah and John learned to address their differences constructively. The team leader acted as a mediator, assisting them in finding solutions that satisfied both parties. As a result, team communication significantly improved, enhancing collaboration. The team completed projects more efficiently, ultimately boosting the company's success.

Case Study 2: Team Building Initiative

In a marketing company, conflicts arose between different departments competing for limited resources. The leader recognized that these conflicts were hampering teamwork and jeopardizing campaign success. To improve the situation, the leader organized a team-building initiative.

During the initiative, team members had the opportunity to exchange ideas in a relaxed environment. The leader facilitated group discussions and team exercises aimed at promoting understanding and collaboration between the departments.

The connections and insights that resulted helped mitigate conflicts. Teams collaborated more effectively, coordinated their activities, and achieved higher campaign performance. This led to increased customer satisfaction and business growth.

Case Study 3: Conflict Coaching

In an educational institution, a conflict arose between a teacher and a school administrative staff member. The leader recognized that the conflict was affecting the school's efficiency and impacting students. Instead of ignoring the conflict, the leader opted to provide conflict coaching for the two individuals involved.

During the coaching process, the individuals received individual support and guidance in resolving their differences. They learned to communicate more effectively and find compromises. The leader established clear expectations for collaboration and conflict resolution.

The improved working relationship between the teacher and the school administrative staff member resulted in smoother school operations. Students benefited from a more harmonious environment and enhanced collaboration. This, in turn, enhanced the school's reputation, attracting more students and positively impacting the institution's success.

These case studies demonstrate how leaders, by recognizing and proactively addressing conflicts, can enhance teamwork and promote business success. The key often lies in a proactive approach, fostering an open communication culture, and being willing to allocate resources for conflict resolution training or coaching.

Conflicts as Opportunities for Improvement

Team conflicts are inevitable, but they do not have to lead to negative outcomes. As a leader, you have the opportunity to use conflicts as opportunities for improvement. Through open communication, neutral mediation, and the application of conflict resolution techniques, you can not only manage conflicts but also strengthen the team and promote business success. Conflicts are a natural part of work life, and with the right tools, you can ensure they lead to positive changes.

Creative Problem-Solving Approaches: The Key to Successful Leadership

In the modern business world, a leader faces numerous challenges and problems. However, the difference between an average and an outstanding leader often lies in how they approach these challenges. Instead of being overwhelmed by problems, successful leaders seek creative problem-solving approaches that enable them to overcome obstacles and foster innovation.

The Importance of Creative Problem-Solving in Leadership

Before delving into specific techniques to promote creative solutions, it is crucial to understand why creativity is essential in leadership:

Innovation

Creative problem-solving fosters innovation, allowing your team or organization to continually evolve and remain competitive.

Flexibility

Creativity enables leaders to adapt to changing circumstances and new challenges, rather than getting stuck in old patterns.

Employee Motivation

By employing creative solutions, you demonstrate to your employees that you are willing to consider their ideas and perspectives, boosting motivation and engagement.

Problem Solving

Creative problem-solving approaches are often more effective in addressing complex problems, as they consider alternative viewpoints and approaches.

Fostering the Creative Thinking Process

Creativity is not an innate ability; it can be developed and nurtured. Here are some approaches to foster the creative thinking process in your leadership role:

Open Communication

Create an environment where ideas and suggestions can be freely exchanged without fear of criticism or rejection.

Promote Diversity

Ensure your team has diverse backgrounds, experiences, and perspectives. Different viewpoints can lead to more creative solutions.

Time and Space for Creativity

Allocate time and space for your team to be creative. This can be achieved through breaks in the workday or specific creativity workshops.

Accepting Mistakes

Emphasize that mistakes are a natural part of the creative process. They are opportunities for improvement and growth.

Creative Problem-Solving Techniques

There are various creative problem-solving techniques that leaders can employ. Here are some proven approaches:

Brainstorming

Brainstorming sessions encourage free idea generation. Encourage your team to voice ideas without criticism, collecting a wide range of suggestions for evaluation.

Design Thinking

Design Thinking is a structured method for solving complex problems. It involves stages such as understanding, observing, idea generation, prototyping, and testing.

Mind Mapping

Mind Mapping is a visual technique where ideas and information are organized in a graphical representation. This can help identify connections and creative solutions.

Reverse Engineering

Consider a problem from a reverse perspective to gain new insights. Imagine the problem is already solved and work backward to figure out how it was achieved.

The Role of the Leader as a Catalyst for Creativity

As a leader, you bear the responsibility of fostering and supporting the creative thinking process within your team. In this chapter, we will discuss how you can act as a catalyst for creativity and inspire your team to seek creative solutions.

Creativity as the Key to Successful Leadership

The ability to find creative solutions to problems is an essential component of successful leadership. By promoting the creative thinking process in your leadership role and employing various creative problem-solving techniques, you can not only overcome obstacles but also foster innovation and growth within your team and organization. Remember that creativity can be learned and nurtured, and utilize it as the key to successful leadership.

Chapter 5

Motivation and Teamwork

Intrinsic vs. Extrinsic Motivation: The Key to Sustainable Leadership

In the realm of leadership, understanding employee motivation is crucial. How people are motivated not only influences their performance but also their engagement, satisfaction, and ultimately, a company's success. In this eBook, we will delve deeply into the topic of "Intrinsic vs. Extrinsic Motivation," showing you as a leader how to comprehend and adeptly utilize these two types of motivation to build a strong and contented team.

Introduction to Intrinsic and Extrinsic Motivation

Before we dive into the details, let's first understand what intrinsic and extrinsic motivation exactly mean:

Intrinsic Motivation

This form of motivation comes from within. Employees are intrinsically motivated when they engage in a task or activity out of personal drive, deriving joy from it, desiring personal growth, or wanting to unfold their skills. The reward lies in the action itself.

Extrinsic Motivation

Extrinsic motivation involves external incentives or rewards that drive employees to complete a task. These can be financial incentives, promotions, recognition, or other external rewards.

The Power of Intrinsic Motivation

In this chapter, we will deeply explore intrinsic motivation and understand why it is so important:

Sustainable Motivation

Intrinsically motivated employees are often motivated in the long term since their motivation isn't dependent on external factors. They are willing to self-motivate and overcome challenges.

Creativity and Innovation

Intrinsically motivated employees tend to be more creative and innovative as they approach their work with passion and curiosity. They are willing to think outside the box and find new solutions.

Higher Satisfaction

Employees who act from intrinsic motivation are generally more satisfied with their work and life in general. They have a higher level of personal well-being.

Lower Turnover Rate

Companies with intrinsically motivated employees tend to have a lower turnover rate because employees find their work meaningful and fulfilling.

Strategies to Foster Intrinsic Motivation

How can you, as a leader, foster intrinsic motivation in your employees? Here are some proven strategies:

Clear Goals and Purpose

Ensure your employees understand the purpose and meaning of their work. Clear goals and a connection to the company's overall vision are crucial.

Provide Autonomy

Allow your employees space to do their work in their own way. Autonomy fosters a sense of control and accountability.

Training and Development

Provide opportunities for professional and personal development. Employees who can grow and improve are more motivated.

Recognition and Praise

Recognition and praise for good work are essential intrinsic motivators. Provide regular positive feedback and show appreciation.

The Significance of Extrinsic Motivation

Extrinsic motivation also has its place in leadership. In this chapter, we will explore how to effectively utilize extrinsic motivation:

Performance Incentives

Rewards such as bonuses, promotions, and incentives can motivate employees to enhance their performance and achieve specific goals.

Recognition and Public Praise

Public recognition among peers and superiors can boost motivation and convey a sense of appreciation.

Competitions and Challenges

Competitions and challenges can inspire employees to give their best and improve their skills.

Flexible Working Conditions

The option for flexible hours or remote work can serve as an extrinsic reward and improve work-life balance.

The Art of Motivation Management

The key to successful leadership often lies in finding the right balance between intrinsic and extrinsic motivation and considering individual needs. In this chapter, we will discuss how you, as a leader, can practice effective motivation management:

Individual Approaches

Every employee is different, and thus, you should develop individual motivation strategies tailored to each person's needs and goals.

Continuous Feedback

Keep the dialogue open with your employees and gather feedback on what motivates them and what doesn't. Adjust your motivation strategies accordingly.

Culture of Appreciation

Create a company culture where recognition and appreciation are deeply ingrained. This promotes both intrinsic and extrinsic motivation.

The Art of Balanced Motivation

Successful employee leadership requires a deep understanding of intrinsic and extrinsic motivation. While intrinsic motivation drives long-term success and engagement, extrinsic motivation can serve as an effective tool for performance enhancement. The art of leadership lies in finding the right balance and developing individual approaches to build a strong and motivated team. By mastering the principles of intrinsic and extrinsic motivation, you will not only enhance your leadership skills but also drive your company's success forward.

Teambuilding - Strategies That Work: How to Build a Strong and Motivated Team as a Leader

Leading a team requires much more than managing tasks and deadlines. A successful leader understands the importance of team building and the role it plays in creating a strong and motivated team. In this eBook, we will extensively explore the topic of "Teambuilding - Strategies That Work" and introduce you to proven methods and approaches that can help you, as a leader, create an effective and harmonious team.

The Importance of Teambuilding in Leadership

Before delving into practical strategies, it is crucial to understand why team building is of paramount importance in leadership:

Enhancing Collaboration

Teambuilding promotes collaboration and the exchange of ideas among team members, leading to more efficient work processes.

Increasing Motivation

A well-coordinated team motivates each other and works collectively towards common goals. Teambuilding contributes to boosting employee motivation.

Conflict Resolution

Teambuilding activities can help identify and address conflicts within the team before they escalate.

Creating a Positive Work Environment

A team that understands each other and collaborates well creates a positive work environment where employees enjoy working.

Teambuilding Strategies That Work

In this chapter, we will explore specific teambuilding strategies that have proven effective in practice:

Teamwork Through Shared Goals

Define clear goals and visions for your team, emphasizing the importance of collaboration in achieving these goals.

Promote Communication

Open and transparent communication is crucial. Encourage team members to share their thoughts and ideas, ensuring information flows freely.

Teambuilding Activities

Organize regular teambuilding activities where team members have the opportunity to get to know each other outside the work environment, building trust.

Define Roles and Responsibilities Clearly

Each team member should know their role in the team and their responsibilities. Clear definitions prevent conflicts and misunderstandings.

Provide Constructive Feedback

Regularly provide constructive feedback to your employees, acknowledging their achievements and highlighting areas for improvement.

Case Studies of Successful Teambuilding Initiatives

In this chapter, we will analyze case studies of successful teambuilding initiatives in various companies and industries. These examples demonstrate how leaders were able to effect positive changes through targeted teambuilding strategies.

The Role of the Leader in Teambuilding

The leader plays a crucial role in teambuilding. In this chapter, we will discuss how you, as a leader, can actively contribute to strengthening your team:

Leading by Example

Be a role model for cooperation, communication, and engagement. Your behavior significantly influences the behavior of your team members.

Fostering Team Members

Recognize the strengths and weaknesses of your team members and promote their individual development.

Conflict Resolution

Leaders should be able to identify and constructively resolve conflicts within the team.

Teambuilding as a Continuous Process

Teambuilding is not a one-time effort but a continuous process. Maintain team spirit through regular activities and efforts.

Measuring the Benefits of Teambuilding

In this section, we will discuss how you can measure the success of your teambuilding initiatives. The right Key Performance Indicators (KPIs) and feedback mechanisms allow you to quantify the benefits of teambuilding and make necessary adjustments.

Teambuilding as the Key to Successful Leadership

Teambuilding is more than just a trend; it is a fundamental aspect of successful employee leadership. A strong and motivated team is the key to a company's success. By applying the strategies and approaches presented here, you can create an environment as a leader where teamwork flourishes, motivation grows, and peak performance is achieved. The art of teambuilding requires time, commitment, and continuous efforts, but the rewards in the form of a strong and effective team are worth it.

Chapter 6

Time Management and Efficiency

Setting Priorities and Making the Most of Your Time: The Key to Effective Leadership

In the role of a leader, effective time utilization and the ability to set clear priorities are crucial. Successfully managing tasks, projects, and teams significantly depends on the ability to optimize time resources and establish the right priorities. In this eBook, we will extensively explore the topic of "Setting Priorities and Making the Most of Your Time" and introduce you to proven strategies and practices that can help you, as a leader, be more productive and achieve better results.

The Importance of Time Management and Prioritization

Before diving into the details, it's essential to understand why time management and prioritization are so crucial for leaders:

Time as a Resource

Time is a limited resource, and how you use it directly impacts your performance and the success of your team and company.

Efficiency and Productivity

Good time management allows you to complete tasks faster and more efficiently, increasing productivity.

Stress Reduction

By prioritizing and using time effectively, you can reduce stress and improve your work-life balance.

Focus on the Essential

Setting priorities helps you focus on truly important tasks and minimize distractions.

Identifying and Combating Time Thieves

In this chapter, we will address how to recognize and counteract time thieves:

Minimizing Distractions

Identify the main sources of distractions in your work environment and take measures to minimize them.

Effective Communication

Learn to use clear and efficient communication methods to avoid misunderstandings and time-consuming meetings.

Setting Priorities

Establish clear priorities for your tasks and projects, focusing on those with the most significant impact.

Utilizing Technology

Use technology to automate repetitive tasks and work more efficiently.

Time Management Tools and Techniques

In this chapter, we will introduce various time management tools and techniques that leaders can use:

To-Do Lists

Create daily or weekly to-do lists to organize your tasks and keep track of them.

Time Blocking

Use time blocks to allocate specific times for particular tasks or projects, minimizing distractions.

Eisenhower Matrix

The Eisenhower Matrix helps you categorize tasks into four categories: urgent and important, important but not urgent, urgent but not important, neither urgent nor important.

Delegation

Delegate tasks to team members when possible, relinquishing responsibility.

The Art of Saying "No"

Leaders are often in high demand and faced with many tasks and requests. In this chapter, we will discuss how you can learn to say "no" when necessary:

Reviewing Priorities

Review your priorities and decline tasks or requests that do not align with your goals and commitments.

Formulating a Polite "No"

Learn to say "no" politely without upsetting or disappointing others.

Delegation

Consider delegating tasks instead of declining them outright.

Time Management as a Leadership Tool

Finally, we will discuss the role of time management as a leadership tool:

Leading by Example

As a leader, you serve as a role model for your employees. Practicing effective time management inspires others to follow your example.

Supporting Employees

Offer your employees resources and training on time management to enhance their efficiency and productivity.

Goal Setting and Monitoring

Set clear goals and monitor progress to ensure your employees are setting the right priorities.

Time Management as the Key to Successful Leadership

Time management and prioritization are essential skills for leaders. By effectively utilizing your time and setting clear priorities, you will not only become more productive but also a more effective and inspiring leader for your team. Time is a precious resource, and how you use it significantly influences your success as a leader. With the strategies and techniques presented here, you can improve your time management and elevate your leadership skills to a higher level.

Delegating: How to Effectively Distribute Tasks and Lead Your Team to Success

Delegating is one of the essential skills that a leader should master. Successfully assigning tasks to team members is not only crucial for an organization's efficiency but also for the development and motivation of employees. In this eBook, we will extensively explore the topic of "Delegating: How to Effectively Distribute Tasks" and introduce you to proven strategies and techniques to master this crucial leadership skill.

The Importance of Delegating in Leadership

Before delving into the details, it's important to understand why delegating is of paramount importance in leadership:

Efficiency and Productivity

Delegating allows tasks to be completed more efficiently by distributing them according to employees' skills and strengths.

Employee Development

Through delegation, employees can acquire new skills and progress, enhancing their motivation and commitment to the company.

Focus on Strategic Tasks

Leaders can concentrate on strategic decisions and long-term goals by delegating, instead of getting involved in operational details.

Time Savings

Delegating enables leaders to save time for more crucial tasks and strategic thinking.

Challenges of Delegating

Before you start delegating, it's important to recognize that there are challenges and obstacles:

Fear of Losing Control

A common obstacle is the fear that delegated tasks might not be performed as well as if the leader did them personally.

Lack of Trust

A leader must have trust in employees' abilities to successfully delegate tasks.

Task Identification

Identifying the right tasks that can be delegated often requires precise analysis and planning.

Communication

Clear communication of expectations and requirements is crucial for the delegation process.

Mastering the Art of Delegating

In this chapter, we will explore the steps and techniques to successfully master delegating:

Identifying Tasks

Start by identifying tasks and responsibilities that can be delegated, requiring a careful analysis of your own work and your employees' skills.

Selecting the Right Person

Consider your employees' skills, experiences, and interests to choose the right person for each task.

Setting Clear Expectations

Clearly communicate the results you expect and ensure employees understand the task and its significance.

Providing Resources

Ensure employees have the necessary resources and information to successfully complete the task.

Transferring Responsibility

Delegate not only tasks but also the responsibility for their successful implementation. Allow employees the freedom to make decisions.

Offering Support and Feedback

Support employees throughout the delegation process, providing assistance and feedback as needed.

Benefits of Delegating

The benefits of delegating are diverse and have positive impacts on both the leader and the entire team:

Leadership Development

Delegating allows leaders to develop their own skills and those of their employees.

Employee Motivation

Employees feel motivated and valued when entrusted with responsibility and autonomy.

Efficiency Enhancement

Delegating allows tasks to be completed faster and more efficiently by assigning them to individuals with the right skills.

Team Strengthening

A well-functioning team collaborates more effectively and productively, promoting the organization's success.

The Role of the Leader in the Delegation Process

The leader plays a crucial role in the delegation process. Here are some key aspects:

Building Trust

Trust your employees and their abilities to successfully carry out delegated tasks.

Feedback and Recognition

Provide regular feedback and recognition for good work, supporting employees' ongoing development.

Taking Responsibility

As a leader, you ultimately bear responsibility for the results of the delegated tasks.

Communication

Keep communication open and transparent to ensure clear goals and expectations.

Optimizing the Delegation Process

Finally, we will discuss how to optimize and continuously improve the delegation process:

Review and Reflection

Take time to reflect on the delegation process, evaluating what worked well and what can be improved.

Training and Development

Invest in training and development for yourself and your employees to expand their skills and competencies.

Flexibility

Be willing to adjust and adapt the delegation process as requirements and goals change.

Delegating as the Key to Successful Leadership

Delegating is a crucial skill that leaders should master. By effectively assigning tasks and leveraging the skills of your employees, you can enhance efficiency and promote your team's development and motivation. The delegation process requires patience, practice, and continuous improvement, but the long-term benefits for both you as a leader and your team are well worth it. Become a master of delegation to achieve your goals and lead successfully.

Chapter 7

Change Management and Innovation

Managing Changes in the Company: A Guide for Leaders

Handling changes in the company is one of the crucial tasks for leaders. In a constantly evolving business world, changes are inevitable. How leaders initiate, communicate, and accompany these changes can significantly influence the company's success and the well-being of the employees. In this eBook, we will delve into the topic of "Managing Changes in the Company" and provide leaders with proven strategies and best practices to effectively cope with changes and keep the company on course.

Why Changes in the Company are Essential

Before delving into managing changes, it's important to understand why changes in the company are necessary:

Competitiveness

Companies must continually evolve to remain competitive and keep pace with changing market demands.

Innovation

Changes enable companies to foster new ideas and innovations that lead to growth and progress.

Adaptability

The ability to adapt to changing conditions is crucial for managing crises and seizing opportunities.

Employee Development

Changes can promote employee development, leading to new skills and competencies.

Challenges of Change Management

However, managing changes in the company also brings challenges that need to be recognized and addressed by leaders:

Resistance to Change

Employees might resist changes when they feel uncertain or uncomfortable.

Communication

Communication of changes is crucial, and lack of clarity can lead to misunderstandings and uncertainties.

Employee Motivation

Changes can impact employee motivation, both positively and negatively.

Time and Resources

Implementing changes requires time and resources that need to be carefully managed.

Strategies for Successful Change Management

In this section, we will present proven strategies for successful change management:

Clear Vision and Goals

Define a clear vision for the changes and set specific goals to be achieved.

Communication

Communicate the changes clearly and repeatedly. Ensure employees understand why the changes are necessary and how they will be affected.

Employee Involvement

Actively involve employees in the change process. Provide them with the opportunity to express their thoughts, concerns, and ideas.

Support and Training

Provide support and training for employees to help them adapt to the changes.

Gather Feedback

Continuously collect feedback from employees to assess progress and potential adjustments.

The Role of the Leader in Fostering Innovation and Creativity

The role of the leader is crucial in creating an environment that fosters innovation and creativity. Here are some key aspects:

Leading by Example

Leaders should exemplify creative thinking and be willing to take risks.

Clear Purpose

Define a clear purpose or vision to guide creative thinking and innovation efforts.

Feedback and Recognition

Provide regular feedback and recognition for creative achievements and innovative ideas.

Supporting Implementation

Assist in implementing innovative ideas by providing resources and removing obstacles.

Measuring and Evaluating Innovation and Creativity

It's important to measure and evaluate innovation and creativity. In this chapter, we will discuss how to do this:

Setting Metrics

Define metrics to measure the success of innovation projects.

Seeking Feedback

Gather feedback from employees to evaluate the quality of ideas and the innovation process.

Making Adjustments

Based on the evaluation results, make adjustments to your innovation efforts to ensure their success.

Creating a Culture of Innovation

Finally, we will discuss how to establish a culture of innovation in your company:

Long-term Commitment

Fostering innovation and creativity requires long-term commitment from leaders and employees.

Openness to Change

Be open to changes and adjustments in your innovation strategy as circumstances change.

Rewarding Innovation

Reward creative ideas and successful innovation projects to motivate employees.

Employee Development

Provide training and development opportunities to enhance your employees' skills in innovation and creativity.

Fostering Innovation and Creativity as Engines for Success

Fostering innovation and creativity in the team requires conscious effort and clear leadership. Leaders who actively promote innovation and creativity can not only create innovative solutions and new business opportunities but also increase employee engagement and satisfaction. By applying the strategies and best practices presented here, you can create an environment where your teams can unleash their full innovation potential, leading your company on a successful path.

Chapter 8

Leadership in Practice

Case Studies of Successful Leaders: Lessons from Practice

The world of leadership is diverse and challenging, and there is no one-size-fits-all solution for success. Successful leaders come from various backgrounds and have different approaches to their work. In this article, we will explore case studies of successful leaders from different industries and fields. We will examine their stories, strategies, and lessons from practice to gain insights into the world of successful leadership.

Case Study 1: Elon Musk - The Visionary

Elon Musk is undoubtedly one of the most well-known entrepreneurs and visionaries of our time. He is the co-founder and CEO of companies like Tesla, SpaceX, and Neuralink. His approach to leadership is characterized by his vision and determination.

Visionary Leadership:

Musk has a clear vision for the future and is committed to realizing this vision. He has set Mars as a goal for human colonization and works tirelessly towards achieving it.

Willingness to Take Risks:

Musk is not afraid of risks and has invested his own fortune in his companies, even when facing financial challenges. His willingness to take significant risks has led to groundbreaking innovations.

Passion and Dedication:

Musk is known for his high level of personal dedication and passion for his projects. He is willing to work tirelessly to achieve his goals.

Lesson: A clear vision, willingness to take risks, and passionate dedication can lead to exceptional outcomes.

Case Study 2: Angela Merkel - The Politician of Continuity

Angela Merkel, the former Chancellor of Germany, had a remarkable political career during her long tenure from 2005 to 2021. Her leadership style is characterized by continuity, stability, and willingness to compromise.

Continuity:

Merkel was known for her ability to maintain continuity and stability in times of uncertainty and change. She relied on proven political principles and strategies.

Willingness to Compromise:

Merkel was willing to make compromises and collaborate with various political parties to ensure political stability. She was a master of diplomacy.

Analytical Approach:

Merkel is renowned for her factual and analytical approach to political issues. She makes decisions based on facts and data.

Lesson: Continuity, willingness to compromise, and an analytical approach can be highly beneficial in politics and other areas of leadership.

Case Study 3: Jeff Bezos - The Innovator

Jeff Bezos is the founder and former CEO of Amazon, one of the world's largest technology companies. His leadership style is characterized by innovation, long-term thinking, and customer focus.

Innovation:

Bezos has consistently led Amazon to innovative breakthroughs, from introducing the Kindle to developing Amazon Web Services (AWS).

Long-Term Thinking:

Bezos thinks in long-term horizons and is willing to endure short-term losses to achieve long-term goals.

Customer Focus:

Bezos oriented Amazon towards meeting the needs of customers from the very beginning, creating a culture where customer satisfaction comes first.

Lesson: Innovation, long-term thinking, and customer focus are key components for success in the technology industry and beyond.

Case Study 4: Malala Yousafzai - The Activist

Malala Yousafzai is a Pakistani activist and the youngest recipient of the Nobel Peace Prize. Her leadership style is characterized by courage, determination, and dedication to education.

Courage:

Malala courageously advocated for the right to education for girls in Pakistan, despite the danger to her own life.

Determination:

Despite an assassination attempt on her, Malala continued her efforts for education and the rights of girls and women.

Global Impact:

Malala initiated a global movement for education and girls' rights, inspiring millions of people.

Lesson: Courage, determination, and the pursuit of a higher cause can be a powerful driving force for positive change.

Case Study 5: Warren Buffett - The Investor

Warren Buffett, Chairman and CEO of Berkshire Hathaway, is one of the most successful investors of all time. His leadership style is characterized by wise financial strategy, humility, and long-term thinking.

Smart Investments:

Buffett is known for his wise investment decisions and his ability to identify companies that will be successful in the long run.

Humility:

Despite being one of the richest people in the world, Buffett remains humble and lives a modest lifestyle.

Long-Term Thinking:

Buffett thinks in decades, not quarters, and prefers long-term investments.

Lesson: Smart financial strategies, humility, and long-term thinking are key components for success in the financial sector.

Case Study 6: Oprah Winfrey - The Media Mogul

Oprah Winfrey is one of the most influential media personalities in the world and a successful entrepreneur. Her leadership style is characterized by empathy, authenticity, and social engagement.

Empathy:

Oprah is known for her empathy and ability to empathize with the feelings and needs of other people.

Authenticity:

She remains true to herself and is authentic in her appearance and interaction with her audience.

Social Engagement:

Oprah has been involved in social and humanitarian causes, using her platform to address important societal issues.

Lesson: Empathy, authenticity, and social engagement can help establish strong connections with other people and bring about positive changes.

Conclusion: Lessons from Successful Leaders

The case studies of successful leaders demonstrate that there is no one-size-fits-all approach to successful leadership. Each person has their own unique style and strengths. However, there are some common lessons that can be drawn from these case studies:

- A clear vision and determination are crucial for success.

- Willingness to take risks can lead to groundbreaking innovations.

- Continuity, willingness to compromise, and an analytical approach are advantageous in politics.

- Innovation, long-term thinking, and customer focus are key to success in the technology industry.

- Courage, determination, and the pursuit of a higher cause can drive positive changes.

- Smart financial strategies, humility, and long-term thinking are significant in the financial sector.

- Empathy, authenticity, and social engagement can help establish strong connections with other people.

These lessons can assist leaders in developing their own approaches and becoming more successful. It's important to emphasize that leadership is an ongoing journey, and there is always room for personal and professional growth.

Tips for Continuous Development as a Leader

The role of a leader is demanding and requires continuous development to be successful. The business world is constantly changing, and leaders must adapt to new challenges and developments. In this article, we will present to you some essential tips for continuous development as a leader. These tips can help you continuously improve your skills and qualities as a leader, enhancing your professional success.

Tip 1: Self-Reflection

One of the most important skills a leader should develop is the ability to self-reflect. Take regular time to contemplate your strengths and weaknesses, analyze your past experiences, and reconsider your professional goals. Reflect on what you have done well and what you can improve. Self-reflection helps you better understand yourself and work consciously on your personal development.

Tip 2: Willingness to Learn

The willingness to continuously learn and adapt to new information and trends is crucial for leadership development. Be open to new ideas, attend training sessions and seminars, read professional literature, and look for opportunities to expand your knowledge and skills. The business world is constantly changing, and only through continuous learning can you stay up-to-date.

Tip 3: Networking

A strong professional network can provide you with valuable resources and support. Connect with colleagues, other leaders, and industry experts. Participate in professional events, conferences, and networking sessions. A well-developed network can not only help you solve challenges but also open up new career opportunities.

Tip 4: Seek Feedback

Feedback is an invaluable tool for development. Regularly ask for feedback from employees, colleagues, and supervisors. Be open to constructive criticism and use it to improve your skills and work methods. Seeking feedback also shows your employees that you are willing to listen and improve, which can enhance your reputation as a leader.

Tip 5: Time Management

Effective time management is crucial for a leader's success. Learn to use your time efficiently by setting priorities, delegating tasks, and focusing on the most important responsibilities. Avoid wasting time on unnecessary meetings or distractions, and utilize technologies and tools to optimize your work processes.

Tip 6: Emotional Intelligence

Emotional intelligence is crucial for leaders. It enables you to recognize and control your own emotions and understand

and respond appropriately to the emotions of your employees. Through emotional intelligence, you can strengthen relationships, resolve conflicts, and create a supportive work environment.

Tip 7: Employee Development

Developing your employees is a crucial task as a leader. Take the time to recognize your employees' skills and potentials and support their professional development. Offer training, mentoring, and coaching to help them succeed. By investing in your employees' development, you strengthen your team and promote their loyalty and engagement.

Tip 8: Communication

Clear and effective communication is a key skill for leaders. Improve your communication skills, both in writing and orally. Ensure that you communicate your expectations and goals clearly, actively listen, and make sure your messages are understood. Good communication promotes collaboration and trust within your team.

Tip 9: Leadership Ethics

Leaders should demonstrate strong ethics and moral integrity. Always act ethically and set high standards for your behavior and that of your employees. Be a role model for ethical conduct and ensure that your decisions and actions align with your company's values and principles.

Tip 10: Work-Life Balance

The work of a leader can be demanding and stressful. It is important to maintain a healthy work-life balance to avoid burnout. Schedule regular breaks and downtime to relax and recharge your energy. Set realistic expectations for yourself and your team, and delegate tasks when possible.

Continuous development as a leader is a lifelong process. By following these tips and actively working on your professional development, you can enhance your leadership qualities and be successful in the long run. Acknowledge your strengths and weaknesses, learn from your experiences, and be willing to adapt to new challenges. Leadership development is not only beneficial for your career but also for the people you lead and your organization as a whole.

Conclusion

The Significance of Value-Based Leadership

Leaders play a crucial role in organizations and businesses of all kinds. Their decisions, behavior, and values directly influence the culture and success of their organizations. In recent years, value-based leadership has emerged as one of the most effective and sustainable forms of leadership. In this article, we have examined the significance of value-based leadership in depth, shedding light on how it impacts the work environment, employee satisfaction, and ultimately, business success.

What is Value-Based Leadership?

Before delving into the significance of value-based leadership, it is important to understand what this term means. Value-based leadership is rooted in a clear set of ethical and moral values that form the foundation for a leader's decisions and actions. These values can be the leader's personal beliefs or derived from the values and principles of the organization they work for.

The fundamental characteristics of value-based leadership are:

1. Authenticity:

Leaders practicing value-based leadership act in alignment with their values and demonstrate authentic behavior. They remain true to themselves and encourage others to do the same.

2. Transparency:

Value-based leaders are open and transparent in their communication. They share information and decision-making processes, thereby fostering trust within their organization.

3. Empathy:

They show compassion and understanding for the needs and concerns of their employees. They are willing to listen and comprehend the perspectives of others.

4. Accountability:

Value-based leaders take responsibility for their actions and decisions. They acknowledge their mistakes and seek solutions.

5. Community:

They promote a sense of belonging and create a positive work environment where employees feel supported and respected.

The Impact of Value-Based Leadership

Value-based leadership can have a transformative effect on organizations and teams. Here are some of its key impacts:

1. Positive Organizational Culture:

Value-based leadership contributes to creating a positive organizational culture centered around ethical principles and moral values. This culture promotes trust, respect, and integrity within the organization. Employees feel comfortable in an environment where they know their leaders make ethical decisions and adhere to them.

2. Employee Engagement and Satisfaction:

Leaders who practice value-based leadership show genuine interest in their employees. This engagement fosters a strong bond between leader and employee, leading to higher employee satisfaction and loyalty. Employees working in a value-based environment are generally more motivated and engaged.

3. Ethics and Integrity:

Value-based leadership promotes ethical behavior and integrity within the organization. Employees are encouraged to make ethical decisions and adhere to moral principles. This contributes to building an ethically responsible company that is successful in the long term.

4. Innovation and Creativity:

A value-based leadership culture can foster innovation and creativity. Employees who feel respected and supported are more willing to present new ideas and develop innovative solutions. This can help gain a competitive advantage and promote a company's growth.

5. Sustainable Success:

Value-based leadership is a crucial factor for long-term and sustainable success. Companies that integrate ethical principles and moral values into their business practices are less susceptible to scandals or ethical violations. This helps maintain the trust of customers, investors, and the public, ensuring long-term growth.

Challenges of Value-Based Leadership

Although value-based leadership offers numerous benefits, there are challenges associated with this type of leadership. Here are some of the most common challenges:

1. Consistency:

Value-based leadership requires consistency. Leaders must live their values consistently in all situations and decisions. Maintaining this consistency can be challenging, especially in stressful or challenging times.

2. Conflicts:

Value-based leadership can lead to conflicts if a leader's values clash with the values of other employees or stakeholders. It is important to resolve conflicts in a constructive manner and promote open dialogue.

3. External Pressure:

Leaders may face external pressure that influences their ability to practice value-based leadership. This pressure can range from financial incentives to political influences. It requires determination and resilience to stay true to one's values despite external influences.

4. Communication and Training:

To create a value-based leadership culture, leaders need to communicate values and expectations clearly. This often requires training and educational programs to ensure all employees understand and accept these values.

Developing Value-Based Leadership

Developing value-based leadership requires time, commitment, and self-reflection. Here are some steps leaders can take to develop their leadership skills in this direction:

1. Identifying Personal Values:

The first step in value-based leadership is identifying and defining personal values. Reflect on what values are important to you and how they influence your behavior and decisions.

2. Integrating Values into Leadership Culture:

Leaders should integrate their personal values into the leadership culture of their organization. This can be done through clear communication, training, and the creation of policies and procedures that reflect these values.

3. Self-Reflection and Continuous Development:

Leaders should practice regular self-reflection, analyzing their actions and decisions in light of their values. Where are they successful, and where is there room for improvement? Continuous development is crucial.

4. Fostering a Value-Based Culture:

Leaders should foster a value-based culture where ethical behavior and moral values are celebrated. This can be achieved through recognizing and rewarding employees who live these values and creating opportunities for discussions and exchanges about values.

5. Leading by Example:

Finally, leaders should lead by example in value-based leadership. They should demonstrate their values through their own behavior and consistently adhere to ethical principles. Through their own example, they can inspire and motivate others to do the same.

Case Studies of Successful Value-Based Leadership

To illustrate the significance of value-based leadership, let's look at some case studies of successful leaders who have placed their values at the core of their leadership.

Case Studies of Future Leadership: Challenges and Opportunities

Challenges for Future Leaders

Technological Disruption:

One of the major challenges for future leaders is technological disruption. Advances in areas such as artificial intelligence, automation, and big data are fundamentally changing how businesses operate. Leaders must understand these technologies and integrate them into their business strategies while ensuring employees acquire the necessary skills to thrive in a digital world.

Diversity and Inclusion:

Workforce diversity is becoming a reality in many companies. Future leaders must effectively lead diverse teams and ensure all employees feel valued and respected. This requires understanding cultural differences and creating inclusive work environments.

Agility and Adaptability:

The business world is changing faster than ever before. Future leaders need to be agile and adaptable to keep up with changing market conditions. This demands the ability to quickly respond to new information, take risks, and adjust strategies.

Ethics and Social Responsibility:

Society increasingly expects ethical behavior and social responsibility from companies and their leaders. Leaders must make ethical decisions and ensure their organizations make a positive contribution to society. This may involve addressing challenges such as environmental conservation, social justice, and ethical business practices.

Globalization:

Globalization has interconnected the business world. Leaders must operate in a global environment, understand international markets, and collaborate with teams from different parts of the world. This requires intercultural competence and the ability to communicate globally.

Opportunities for Future Leaders

Innovation and Creativity:

One of the exciting opportunities for future leaders is fostering innovation and creativity within their organizations. Advances in technology and communication allow for the rapid development and implementation of new ideas and approaches. Leaders can create a culture of innovation, driving their organizations forward.

Talent Development:

Developing and nurturing talent will be a key task for future leaders. They have the opportunity to recognize and develop their employees' skills and leadership potential. This can help retain talented employees and enhance team performance.

Sustainability and Social Responsibility:

The increasing demand for sustainability and social responsibility provides leaders with the opportunity to effect positive change within their organizations. They can develop sustainability strategies, promote ethical business practices, and have a positive impact on the community.

Digitization and Efficiency Enhancement:

Digitization offers the opportunity to optimize business processes and enhance efficiency. Leaders can use technology to automate workflows, analyze data, and make better decisions. This can increase a company's competitiveness.

Leadership and Culture Creation:

The opportunity to shape a positive corporate culture and lead employees is one of the central opportunities for future leaders. They can develop an inspiring vision, lead by example, and create a supportive work environment. This contributes to employee satisfaction, loyalty, and performance.

Strategies for Addressing Challenges and Seizing Opportunities

Continuous Learning and Development:

To address the challenges of technological disruption and a changing business world, future leaders should consider continuous learning and development. This may involve participating in training, seminars, and educational programs to keep their skills and knowledge up to date.

Promoting Diversity:

To foster diversity and inclusion within their organizations, leaders should consider training in intercultural competence and creating inclusive work environments. They should also assemble diverse teams and ensure all voices are heard.

Developing Flexibility and Adaptability:

Developing flexibility and adaptability requires practice. Leaders can achieve this by actively seeking new challenges, taking responsibility for changes, and learning from mistakes. It is important to constantly adapt to new situations and respond flexibly to them.

Prioritizing Ethics and Social Responsibility:

Prioritizing ethics and social responsibility requires clear guidelines and principles within the organization. Leaders should exemplify a clear vision for ethical behavior and ensure these values are integrated into all business decisions.

Networking and Collaboration:

The ability to network and collaborate is crucial to benefit from the opportunities of innovation and creativity. Leaders should actively participate in networks, exchange ideas, and form partnerships to develop innovative solutions.

The Future of Leadership

The future of leadership will be shaped by leaders who are willing to face challenges and seize opportunities. These leaders will not only be able to successfully lead their organizations but also effect positive changes in society. The future of leadership is dynamic and exciting, and those who are willing to adapt and learn will succeed.

Printed in Great Britain
by Amazon